This book belongs to....

Small preview of what's inside

Autumn Blessing

Hello Autumn

Hello Autumn

Autumn Colors

Tree-House

Forest Arbres

Fall
Fall Breeze

Before Autumn

Haunted House

Halloween

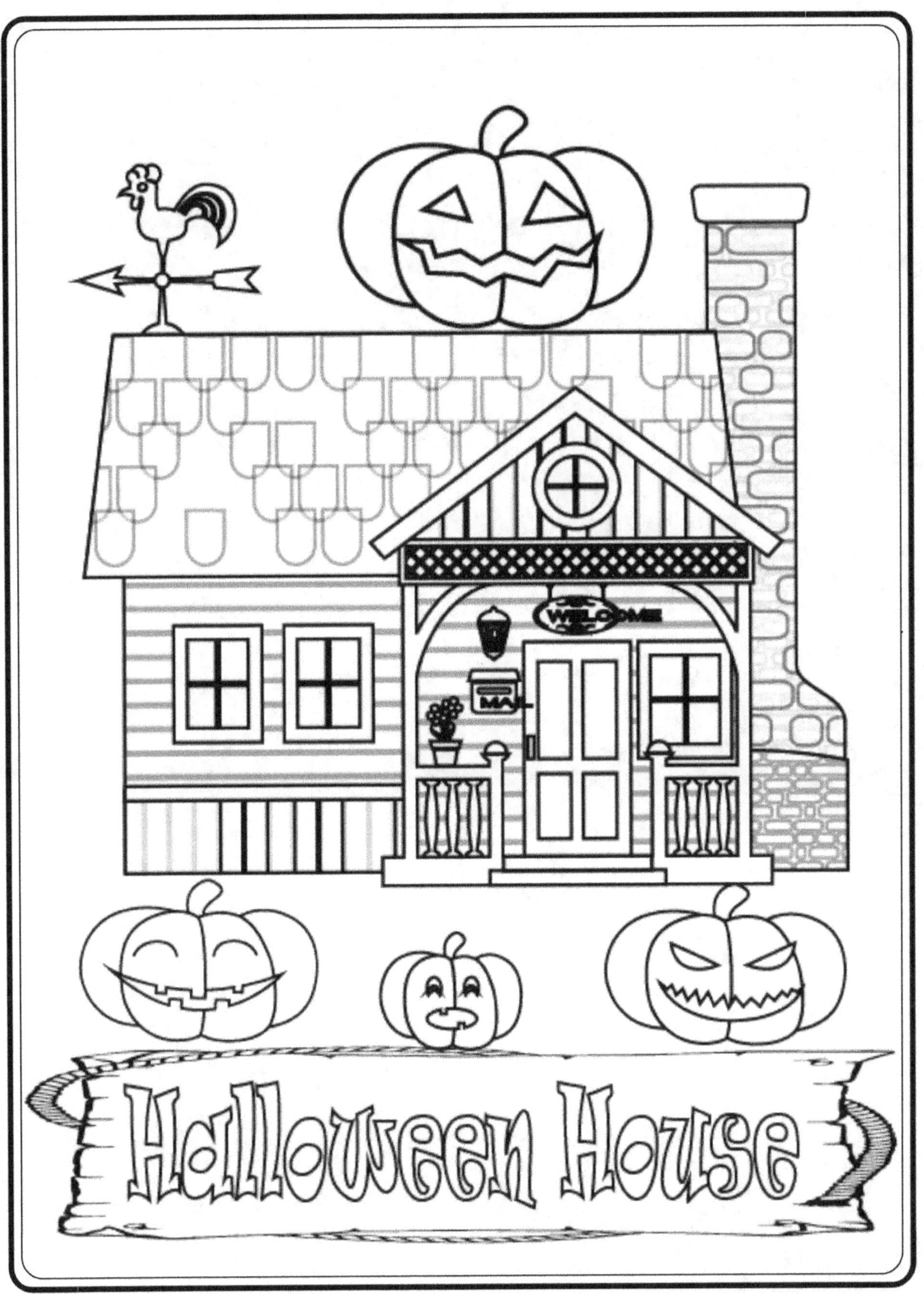

WELCOME
Halloween House

Give Thinks

SUGAR
SALT
Thinks Giving

Happy
Thinks Giving

Thinks Giving

Happy
Thinks Giving

Happy
Thinks Giving

Happy
Thinks Giving

Autumn Cercle

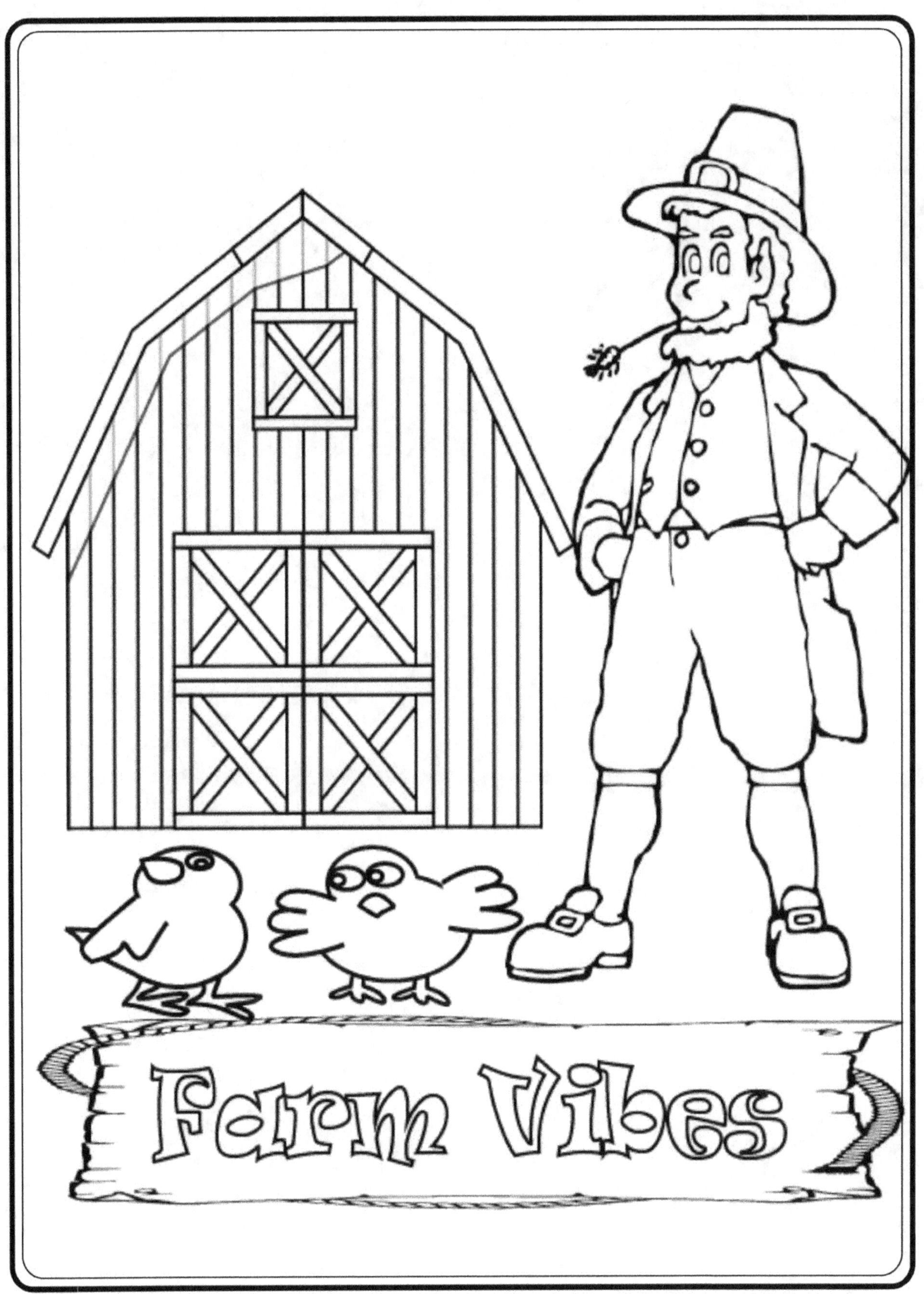

Farm Vibes

Scarecrow

Autumn Embroidery

Autumn Dwarf

Farm Life

Autumn Farm

Autumn Blessing

Cute Teddy

Pre-Autumn

Garden Gnome

Hello Cat

Gift Day

Cristmas

Cristmas

Flowers

Autumn

HELLO AUTUMN

Autumn

www.ingramcontent.com/pod-product-compliance
Lightning Source LLC
Chambersburg PA
CBHW081418250726
48654CB00013B/1746